Healing the Past Through the Present

Gia

Published by Rooted Hound Press LLC
Vienna, New Jersey
www.rootedhoundpress.com

ISBN: 978-1-969687-04-4

Cover design by Rooted Hound Press
Printed in the United States of America

For permissions or inquiries, contact:
support@rootedhoundpress.com

Dedication

For those who came before us,
and for those who will come after —
may we all find peace in the space between.

Prelude — The Curse in the Forest

"Every story has a root, and some roots are tangled in love."

Long ago, in a land where the forest whispered secrets to the wind, there lived a young man — my ancestor — who was known for his kindness and his heart for simple things. He worked hard, laughed often, and spent his evenings at a small tavern at the edge of the woods, where a young woman with eyes like warm amber served ale to weary travelers.

He loved her quietly, the way honest men do, with devotion rather than promises.

One winter night, the kingdom fell into unrest. The King's only daughter — the Princess — wandered into the forest and did not return. The King offered a reward to any man who could find her and bring her home: her hand in marriage, and half the royal dowry besides.

Men from every province entered the dark woods, but only one returned — the tavern girl's beloved. He had found the Princess, cold and frightened, and carried her safely to the gates.

The King kept his word. He offered the young man the Princess's hand in marriage. But the man bowed low and said, "Your Majesty, I cannot accept. My heart already belongs to another."

The court gasped. The Princess's cheeks burned red with shame. To be refused by a commoner — it was an insult no royal could bear.

And so, with eyes like embers, she spoke the words that would shape generations:

"Then may love never bring joy to you or your kin. May your house know comfort but never wealth, companionship but never peace, and may every union be haunted by longing that cannot rest."

The forest grew still. The young man left with the woman he loved, and together they built a family, not knowing that her words would echo through time — through struggle, through heartache, through me.

Preface — Remembering Forward

Some stories live inside families like whispers. They pass quietly from one generation to the next — not through books or records, but through feeling. A heaviness here, a struggle there, a sense that something began long before us and is still waiting to be understood.

For as long as I can remember, my family carried one of those stories. They called it *the curse*.

It began, they said, with a proud man who refused a royal hand, a princess who felt humiliated, and a curse that doomed his family line to struggle and heartbreak. I used to think it was just a tale — something said to explain why life always seemed hard. But over time, I began to feel its presence, not as superstition, but as energy — a story that wanted to be healed.

This book is that healing.

It began as a reflection, a way to make peace with the ghosts of my past. But it became more than that — a living conversation with my lineage. A journey through memory, forgiveness, and the realization that time itself can fold and heal through love.

If you have ever carried a story that wasn't entirely yours — if you've ever felt the weight of something old moving through your life — this book is for you.

Together, we will travel backward and forward through the heart, exploring how our present choices can transform the past and open the way for brighter tomorrows.

May these pages remind you that healing does not erase the story — it rewrites its ending.

— **Gia**

Rooted Hound Press, 2025

Chapter 1 — The Family That Carried the Curse

"Every family carries a story that believes it must be true."

The Whisper at the Kitchen Table

In my family, stories were told the way prayers are said—quietly, often, and with a hint of fear. When things went wrong, my mother would sigh and say, "It's the curse, you know. The Kern curse."

She believed in signs: a cup that cracked on its own, a bird that hit the window, dreams that foretold bad news. At the table, her voice would grow certain, trying to convince my father that misfortune had followed him from Germany all the way to America. He never argued loudly. He'd stare into the amber swirl of his drink, jaw set, eyes far away. Sometimes he'd lift the glass and say only, *"Maybe so."*

Two highballs would stand between them like twin lanterns—hers on the table, his in his hand—glowing softly as they revisited the same weary debate: fate or failure, love or luck, blame or burden.

Before America

My father had been stationed in Germany just after the war, twenty-three and already divorced—a fact he never told us. My mother was nineteen, engaged to a local *Fußball* player, certain of her future until fate—or someone's will—rewrote it.

Her parents decided she would marry the American sailor. "A better life," they said. "A new beginning." She boarded a ship in 1949 with a suitcase and a broken heart, leaving behind the boy who played soccer and made her laugh. By the time she reached the New World, she'd learned the art of silence.

The Craftsman and the Believer

My father once worked with leather—fine handbags, belts, pieces so carefully stitched that the seams were almost invisible. I've seen the photographs, but I have no memory of the smell of tanned hide or the rhythm of his tools. By the time I was old enough to remember, the tools were packed away. What remained was the man in the chair, the glass in his hand, and the soft hum of my mother's voice filling the room with accusation or prophecy.

Their love became a tug-of-war between reason and superstition. He trusted what he could touch; she trusted what she could sense.

And somewhere between their two worlds, six children grew up learning both languages: the practical and the mystical, the visible and the unseen.

Children of a Story

We never knew where the curse began, only that it was blamed for everything that hurt. When money vanished, when jobs failed, when tempers flared—there it was, the Princess's shadow. Even as a child, I felt it humming underneath ordinary life, like a second heartbeat we could not silence.

It wasn't until years later that I wondered if the true spell had nothing to do with a jealous Princess or an old forest at all. Maybe it was cast the day two young people traded love for duty and drowned their grief in matching glasses of amber light.

Reflection: What We Inherit

Curses don't always come from witches; sometimes they come from wounds left unhealed. My parents carried pain they didn't know how to name, so they called it destiny. I've learned that when love is forced, it fractures—and those fractures echo through generations until someone finally listens.

Affirmation

"I listen to the silence between my parents' words. In that silence, I find compassion. Their story ends in peace through me."

Journaling Prompts

1. What patterns or coping habits have you seen repeated across generations in your family?
2. How did your parents or caregivers explain hardship—through logic, faith, or myth?
3. If you could rewrite one moment of their story with understanding instead of blame, what would change?

Journaling

Journaling

Chapter 2 — The Weight of the Name

"A name is a spell spoken through time."

The Name I Didn't Understand

When I was little, the word *Bohlen* drifted through our house like a forgotten melody. I heard it in bits — my mother's accent curling around it, my father grunting something about "old family." It meant nothing then. I was too busy trying to make sense of the world in front of me to care about the one that came before.

It wasn't until I was nearly grown up, married at seventeen, and already carrying more responsibility than wisdom — that the name came back to me. One evening, my mother mentioned it again, almost wistfully.

"You know, our family was von Bohlen once."

She said it softly, as if the *von* itself were a ghost that might disappear if spoken too loudly. She didn't know exactly what it meant — only that it had something to do with land, with title, with a life that had slipped through generations of hard hands.

By then, she was the only child of two parents long gone, and my father's family was scattered like leaves. No one left to ask. No one left who remembered the details. Just a name, half-remembered, heavy with questions.

Pieces of a Puzzle

My father had grown up without the comfort of knowing his own history. He and his sisters had been placed in an orphanage when he was small — not abandoned, exactly, but set aside while their parents came ahead to America to build a life they could later bring the children into. There was an aunt who watched over them, a kindness I cling to, but the truth is that his earliest years were made of work and waiting.

He told almost nothing of that time, yet sometimes a story would surface through my siblings — how he shoveled coal in winter until his hands blistered, how his father made him earn every kindness. At fifteen he tried to join the Navy; too young. So he found a year's berth with the Merchant Marines — or so my sister swears — and by sixteen he wore a uniform for real. By twenty-three he was in Germany, meeting my mother and setting in motion everything that would become us.

I piece these stories together like scraps of a tapestry missing half its threads. Every time I pull on one, another unravels. That is the weight of an incomplete inheritance — the yearning to know and the ache of never fully knowing.

The Silence Between Generations

I sometimes think the silence around our history was its own kind of inheritance. It taught us to live forward, not backward — to survive without asking too many questions. Yet inside me, curiosity always pressed against that silence, the way a seed presses through soil seeking light.

When I finally looked for the name *Bohlen* in old records, I found fragments — noble lines, barons in distant provinces, and a family crest unlike any I'd seen. It bore a helmet crowned by a pair of curved, red-and-gold striped horns — proud, strange, and unforgettable.

My mother knew what that name meant. She told me more than once that *von Bohlen* was not just a name but a title, and that long ago our family had held land, rank, and privilege. She believed that the curse itself had stolen all of it — that the Princess's anger had not only doomed love and fortune but stripped the family of its rightful inheritance.

Whenever she spoke of it, her eyes would soften, shadowed by a sadness I didn't yet understand — as if she truly believed we'd been robbed of a life we deserved. In her mind, the curse explained everything: why we struggled, why my father's branch carried no title, why the weight of "what might have been" still hung in the air. And I began to wonder if that sense of loss, handed down like an heirloom, was the truest inheritance of all.

What a Name Can Carry

To some, a name is only sound. To me, it became an echo of belonging I didn't have. It carried all the questions my parents never answered, all the history my mother hinted at, all the work my father never spoke of. It held pride and shame, promise and loss. And within that name I began to see the outline of my own searching — for meaning, for worth, for a sense of where I fit in the long story that started long before I was born.

Maybe that is what a name truly is: a bridge between what was forgotten and what still remembers.

Reflection — The Hunger to Know

We imagine that knowing our lineage will give us roots, but sometimes it only reveals how deep the hunger runs. The truth is, not all histories can be recovered. Some must be re-dreamed. In choosing to heal, I realized that I don't need every document or every tale. What matters is the intention I place behind the name — to let it stand not for loss, but for endurance.

Affirmation

"Though I may never know the full story, I carry its light forward. My name is not a burden; it is a promise to remember with love."

Journaling Prompts

1. What parts of your family history remain a mystery to you?

2. How does not knowing affect your sense of identity?

3. If you could choose what your family name *means* from this day forward, what would you decide?

Journaling

Journaling

Chapter 3 — Love and Lack: The Dual Curse

"Some inherit jewels, others inherit debts. We inherited a pattern."

Two Shadows at the Table

In our home, love and struggle always came in the same breath. If there was laughter, it was followed by worry; if there was tenderness, it was edged with fatigue. My parents' marriage was a seesaw that never quite balanced — one side weighted with affection, the other with fear that everything could vanish by morning.

When bills piled up, my mother would call it *the curse* again. "See?" she'd tell my father. "It won't ever let us get ahead."

He'd pour another highball, the ice clicking like punctuation in a sentence too familiar to finish. I didn't understand money then, but I understood tension — the kind that hums in the walls and makes even laughter sound nervous.

To me, love looked like endurance. It looked like my mother was staying when she wanted to leave, my father providing when it hollowed him out. It looked like two people clinging to each other because letting go would mean losing the only proof they had that they'd ever been chosen.

The Arithmetic of Survival

I learned early that affection could not exist without cost. If we had enough to pay a bill, someone would get sick. If my father's overtime came through, the car would break down. Good fortune never arrived alone; it always brought its debt collector.

Some nights, after the arguing faded, I'd lie awake counting — not sheep, but worries of rent, groceries, the overdue notice on the counter. Even as a child, I kept mental ledgers, as though keeping track might keep disaster at bay.

Looking back, I see that both lived inside scarcity, not just of money, but of ease. They didn't know how to receive without bracing for loss. And that's how the curse keeps itself alive — by convincing each generation that joy must be repaid with suffering.

Echoes in My Own Life

I carried that arithmetic into adulthood without realizing it. Married at seventeen, I mistook responsibility for love and struggle for meaning. Whenever life felt peaceful, I'd find a way to disrupt it — as if comfort were suspicious, as if some part of me still believed happiness would invite punishment.

I worked too hard, gave too much, apologized for wanting more. The pattern of love and lack had rooted itself deep — not just in finances, but in my heart. Even my moments of abundance felt temporary, borrowed, undeserved.

It would take years before I saw that I was reenacting a family script, one written in the language of survival instead of trust.

When I Began to Question

The first crack in that belief came quietly. One evening, I realized that my parents' struggle had not been fate — it had been *familiarity*. They repeated what they knew: that love meant sacrifice and safety meant scarcity. I began to wonder what would happen if I stopped repeating it.

Could I allow love without earning it? Could I accept enough without fearing the loss that followed?

Healing, I discovered, isn't about undoing the past; it's about ending the performance of it.

Reflection — Rewriting the Ledger

Love and money are both forms of energy — both ask whether we feel worthy to receive. When a family lives long enough under a shadow of lack, even affection becomes currency. To break that pattern, we must stop measuring our value by how much we endure.

Affirmation

"I release the belief that joy must be paid for. Love is not a debt. Abundance is not a threat. I am safe to receive both."

Journaling Prompts

1. What were you taught — directly or indirectly — about money, love, and worthiness?

2. Do you find yourself expecting loss to follow joy? When did that belief begin?

3. What would "abundance" look like if it were measured in peace instead of possessions?

Journaling

Journaling

Chapter 4 — The Turning: Seeing the Curse Differently

"Every spell breaks the moment you understand it."

The Long Belief

For most of my life, I believed the curse was real. Not just a story, not a metaphor — *real*. I prayed against it, whispered words of protection over my home, and begged for release from whatever force had tangled itself through our bloodline.

Every month, every setback, every broken dream seemed to prove it was still working. If a relationship faltered, it was the curse. If money vanished, it was the curse again. Even my own sadness felt inherited, as if I were fulfilling an old contract I'd never signed.

For decades, I said the same prayer: *"Let it end with me."* I meant it with all my heart. I wanted freedom for my children, for their children — for anyone who would bear our name after me.

The Quiet Shift

Then, slowly, something began to change. I started reading, meditating, and asking questions I'd once been afraid to ask. At first, it felt like disobedience — to doubt the curse was to doubt my mother, the stories, the very structure of our family's pain. But curiosity is its own kind of prayer, and mine was finally being answered.

I realized that what I'd been calling a *curse* might actually be an *invitation* — a mirror showing me where love had been withheld and how fear had disguised itself as fate. The pattern wasn't supernatural; it was emotional, human, and heartbreakingly familiar. It lived in choices, in silence, in beliefs carried forward without question.

The moment I saw that, the power shifted. The curse hadn't been hunting me; I had been feeding it.

Learning a New Language

Spirituality taught me that energy follows attention. All those years of praying against the curse, I was still turning toward it — naming it, feeding it, believing in its strength. The day I stopped fighting and started listening was the day everything began to loosen.

I began to thank my ancestors instead of fearing them. I lit candles not to banish darkness, but to honor the light they could never fully see. In meditation, I'd sometimes whisper: *"I understand now. You were doing the best you could."* The prayer changed from *"Let it end with me"* to *"Let it heal through me."*

Reflection — Reframing the Curse

A curse is only a story we've forgotten how to read. When we see it clearly, it becomes a teacher. Mine taught me about choices. Choices that can break the cycle not by rejecting my family's past, but by meeting it with compassion. Healing doesn't erase what was; it transforms its meaning.

Affirmation

"I no longer fight my past. I listen, I learn, I love. What once felt like a curse now guides me home."

Journaling Prompts

1. When did you first start questioning the stories you grew up believing?

2. What patterns began to shift once you viewed them through understanding instead of fear?

3. How does your definition of *healing* differ from *ending*?

Journaling

Journaling

Chapter 5 — The Work of Healing

"Awareness is the spark; practice is the flame that keeps it alive."

When Awareness Became Practice

Realizing the curse wasn't real magic, but just an inherited belief, didn't free me overnight. The moment of understanding is only the doorway; walking through it takes time. At first, I thought enlightenment would feel dramatic. Like bells ringing and chains falling. Instead, it felt quiet. Ordinary. Like getting up one morning and deciding to breathe differently.

Healing began with small, almost invisible choices: to pause before reacting, to notice the old fear rising in my chest and choose calm instead, to stop repeating the stories that began with *"we never get ahead"* or *"things always fall apart."*

Each choice was a thread pulled from the old tapestry, loosening the weaves of what once held me tight.

Listening to the Body

I learned that healing isn't only of the mind. The body remembers everything: the poverty of breath during arguments, the tightening in the stomach when money ran short, the way the shoulders curled inward around unspoken worry. When I began to meditate, I found those memories living inside me like echoes.

Some days I'd place a hand over my heart and whisper, *"You're safe now."* Other days, I'd cry without knowing why, as if my cells were finally allowed to exhale.

Ayurveda, breathwork, walks in the sun, long baths scented with lavender—none of it was complicated. Each practice said the same thing in a different language: you can choose peace in this body, in this moment.

Making Peace with the Past

As I softened, so did the images of my parents. I stopped seeing them as victims of a curse and began to see two wounded souls doing the best they could with what they knew. I wrote letters I never sent—one to my mother, one to my father—thanking them for the strength that came from their survival. When I lit candles for them, I didn't ask for protection anymore; I offered forgiveness.

That's when the heaviness around our name began to lift. Not because anything in history changed, but because my perception did. The story was the same—only the storyteller was healing.

Learning to Receive

For the first time, I practiced receiving without guilt. Compliments. Rest. Small luxuries like a cup of tea I didn't rush through. It felt awkward at first, almost indulgent. But that's how you teach a nervous system raised on scarcity that it's safe to relax.

Abundance doesn't always arrive as money. Sometimes it's the quiet certainty that you don't have to earn love, that it's already yours. That realization felt like the actual breaking of the curse.

Reflection — The Everyday Miracle

Healing isn't an event; it's a daily relationship with truth. Each time we choose compassion over criticism, presence over avoidance, we mend a small tear in the lineage. The miracle isn't that the past changes, it's that we no longer must carry it the same way.

Affirmation

"I honor the work of healing in all its small, steady forms. Each breath of peace I take frees those who came before me. The line is lighter because I chose love."

Journaling Prompts

1. What daily habits or thoughts keep you connected to old patterns of fear or scarcity?

2. How does your body signal safety or stress? What helps it soften?

3. In what small ways can you practice receiving today—without guilt or justification?

Journaling

Journaling

Chapter 6 — The Ancestral Bridge

"When one generation finds peace, the others finally rest."

The Knowing

My mother always seemed to know things before they happened. She'd dream of a storm before it arrived, sense when someone was sick, feel a heaviness in her chest when bad news was near. So when she said, *"I think it's my time,"* I believed her.

She didn't say it with fear. She said it the way someone might announce that the long day was finally over and she was ready to go home. At the time, I thought it was just her superstition again — another of her omens, another way of turning life into prophecy. But now I see it differently.

She wasn't predicting her death. She was *choosing* release. Not from this world, but from a life she had never truly been free to live.

The Weight She Carried

My mother lived as though happiness were something other people were given at birth, a gift she had been passed over for. Her laughter was quick but fleeting, like sunlight that vanished before you could step into it. She'd sit at the kitchen table, cigarette smoke curling between her fingers, staring at nothing — as if the walls themselves reminded her of the life she might have had.

Looking back now, I realize she felt trapped: by duty, by disappointment, by the unending repetition of struggle. And though her death was called "natural," I believe she willed herself into rest. Her spirit had grown too tired to pretend anymore.

I used to wish she'd fought harder to stay, but now I wish she'd been given something worth staying for — a sense of beauty, of possibility, of belonging to her own life. She did the best she could with what she knew, and what she knew was pain. If she'd had the help, the tools, the understanding that I've since found, she could have made her life beautiful. I see that now, and the seeing itself is part of the healing.

The Grief That Taught Me

For years, I grieved her as the woman she was. Now I grieve for the woman she *never got to be*. The one who might have painted, or danced in her kitchen, or believed she deserved happiness simply because she was alive.

That kind of grief doesn't end; it transforms. It becomes a purpose. Every time I choose joy, I feel like I'm choosing it for her, too. Every time I forgive myself, I sense her sighing somewhere in relief.

Sometimes, when I light a candle for her, I whisper: *"You can rest now. I'll finish what you started."*

The Bridge Between Worlds

The older I get, the more I understand that healing doesn't end with the living. When we free ourselves from patterns of suffering, we free those who came before us, too. Energy doesn't disappear; it evolves. I like to believe that each breath of peace I take sends a ripple through time, touching her, touching them all — a thread of light mending what once tore us apart.

My mother gave me the story; I'm giving her the ending. And somewhere, I imagine, she's smiling — not because I broke the curse, but because I finally understood it.

Reflection — Love Beyond Time

Grief is not the opposite of love; it is love's continuation. When we grieve with awareness, we turn sorrow into wisdom. Our ancestors live in that wisdom, not as ghosts but as guides — the quiet knowing that what once hurt can now be held gently.

Affirmation

"I honor my mother's journey with compassion. I carry her light forward, not her pain. In healing myself, I have given her the peace she longed for."

Journaling Prompts

1. What unfulfilled dreams or emotions do you sense your parents carried?

2. How can you honor those dreams through your own choices and joy?

3. When you imagine your ancestors watching you heal, what do you hope they feel?

Journaling

Journaling

Chapter 7 — The Language of Light

"Love never dies; it just learns new ways to speak."

When the Silence Changed

After my mother passed, my life felt unbearably quiet. I was already married and out of the house, but it was as though a frequency had gone missing — a sound I didn't know I'd depended on until it was gone. Grief doesn't only echo through the place we lose someone; it echoes through the places they once existed inside us.

That silence might have swallowed me completely, if not for my mother-in-law. She seemed to sense the emptiness before I could name it. With the gentlest heart, she tried to fill the space — not with words, but with acts of love. She taught me how to sew, gave me my first sewing machine, and sent me home with stacks of fabric. Thread by thread, I began stitching something that felt like healing. Each piece of cloth was a small prayer — proof that creation could exist where loss had been.

Looking back, I think she was the first person to show me that love doesn't die; it simply changes its form. My mother had left me with stories; my mother-in-law gave me hands that could turn them into something beautiful.

Dreams Like Visits

Not long after she died, I dreamt of her standing in the yard, wearing the blue sweater she loved. She looked young again, her face unlined, her shoulders relaxed. She didn't speak — she just smiled and waved, a simple, wordless gesture that somehow said everything: *I'm okay.*

That dream stayed with me for years. Sometimes I'd wake from it crying, not in sorrow but in gratitude. It was the first time I truly believed that love could travel beyond the veil of form — that healing wasn't limited to this world.

Since then, she has appeared in other ways: through a dragonfly hovering at my window, a breeze that carries warmth even on a cold day, a deep calm that settles in my chest during prayer. I've come to understand that these are her ways of saying hello.

Learning to Listen Differently

When I stopped waiting for a voice and started listening with my heart, I noticed that communication was everywhere. Energy has its own language — subtle but unmistakable. It speaks through repetition, timing, intuition, the sudden knowing that arrives without logic. Some call it imagination. I call it love continuing its conversation.

I used to think I needed proof that she was at peace; now I feel her peace inside me. It's the part of me that no longer fears the past, that breathes more easily, that trusts the unseen.

The Ancestral Choir

Over time, it wasn't just my mother I felt near. It was as though generations gathered behind her — quiet presences, not haunting but humming, reminding me that I carry all of them in my cells. Sometimes, during meditation, I sense them standing behind me, a lineage of souls watching softly as I write, as I heal, as I finally live differently. Their message is simple: *"We're proud of you. Keep going. You are the prayer we could not finish."*

That thought alone fills me with awe. The idea that my small, human acts of forgiveness ripple backward through time, softening what once felt hard and lonely.

Reflection — The Continuation of Love

Death does not end a relationship; it changes its direction. When we listen beyond the noise of fear, we find our loved ones speaking through beauty, synchronicity, and peace. Every healed moment is a word in their language of light — and when we answer with gratitude, the conversation continues.

Affirmation

"Love never leaves; it transforms. I am surrounded by those who came before me, and together we speak the language of light."

Journaling Prompts

1. Have you ever felt a loved one's presence in a way that defied explanation?

2. How do signs or synchronicities make you feel — comforted, uncertain, connected?

3. In what moments do you feel most supported by something unseen?

Journaling

Journaling

Chapter 8 — The Art of Living Whole

"Peace isn't something we find — it's something we allow."

A Different Kind of Listening

These days, I live more slowly. I listen differently now — not for voices or signs, but for the gentle rhythm of life itself. It's as if the years of searching for meaning finally taught me that meaning was never hiding; it was simply quiet.

For so long, I wanted proof — proof that my mother was at peace, proof that the curse had ended, proof that healing was real. Now I understand that the proof is in how I live: in the softness of my mornings, in the way I forgive faster, in the peace that hums beneath the noise of everyday life.

The world still speaks — just not always in words.

The Bridge at Gettysburg

Once, long after my mother had passed, Hubs and I met some friends in Gettysburg for vacation. They were paranormal researchers — "ghost hunters," they called themselves — and they invited us to join them at Sachs Bridge, a place said to hum with echoes of the past.

I remember the night clearly: warm air, the soft creak of the wooden boards under our feet, the hum of cicadas in the distance. While our friends set up their recording equipment and called into the darkness, Hubs wandered down by the river with his fishing gear, content to sit in quiet water and starlight.

We were focused, intent, desperate for a response — and nothing came. But then, out of nowhere, Hubs came tearing up the path, arms full of his gear, muttering, "Nope, nope, nope!" We followed him, startled and laughing, and he finally said, "I was down there minding my own business when I heard someone call my name. I looked — no one was there. Then it came again, louder. That's it — I'm done!"

Even now, that story makes us laugh. But it also reminds me of something sacred: sometimes, when we're straining for a sign, the universe speaks to the one who isn't trying at all. Hubs was in his element — calm, peaceful, open — and in that stillness, the unseen found a way to reach him. He didn't need to *seek* connection; he simply *was* it.

What makes that night even more meaningful is that Hubs had once longed for a sign from his father. When his dad passed — almost two decades before that evening — his mother and brothers each said they'd felt his presence or heard his voice. Hubs, though, never did. He was open-hearted, but he wasn't ready then. I think, in some quiet way, that night at Sachs Bridge was his sign — late, but right on time.

We still don't know who called his name. Maybe it was his father, maybe his best friend and old fishing buddy, or maybe the two of them together, conspiring to give him a good scare. And honestly, it fits them both. If it *was* them, they succeeded — he raced past us like the ground was on fire, and we still laugh about it to this day.

But beneath the laughter, there's something more profound: sometimes love reaches across the veil in the only language we'll hear — humor, surprise, and the shock of being noticed when we least expect it.

It's the same with healing. The moment we stop forcing peace to arrive, it does.

Living from the Center

The woman I am now no longer lives in survival mode. I don't chase what's gone or brace for what's coming. I meet each day where it is, breathing gratitude into the ordinary.

My house is quieter, but not empty. There's a presence in everything — in the flicker of candlelight, the hum of my sewing machine, the scent of lavender from the dried flowers I keep on my desk. These small rituals have become my prayers. They're how I live my love now — grounded, creative, whole.

The curse that once felt like a shadow over my family has become my teacher. It showed me that freedom doesn't come from escaping pain but from transforming it. And in that transformation, I discovered joy that doesn't need permission to exist.

Reflection — The Wholeness of Living

To live whole is not to live without pain. It's to allow light and shadow to coexist without fear. It's to laugh at a memory, cry at another, and understand that both are sacred. Healing isn't about forgetting the past; it's about living so fully in the present that the past no longer defines you.

Affirmation

"I live each day as proof that healing is real. Peace is no longer something I seek — it lives within me. I am whole, and life is beautiful."

Journaling Prompts

1. When was the last time you felt a deep sense of peace, even in an ordinary moment?

2. What does "living whole" mean to you today?

3. How do laughter, creativity, and gratitude help you stay connected to your healing?

Journaling

Journaling

Chapter 9 — The Body Remembers

"The body keeps every whisper until the heart is ready to listen."

Where the Past Lives

Long before we ever speak our pain, the body knows it. It knows the way shoulders lift when we hear an argument, the way the breath shortens when we expect disappointment, the way our stomach tightens before bad news. Every memory leaves an echo, and over time, those echoes build into a language of their own — one written in heartbeat, muscle, and bone.

For years, I mistook those sensations for weakness. When my chest ached, I thought something was wrong with my heart. When my back stiffened, I blamed age or work. It took time to understand that the ache wasn't an injury — it was a memory. My body was holding everything my mind hadn't yet made peace with.

When I began to soften instead of resist, I started to hear what those sensations were saying. Fear sounded like a flutter in my chest. Anger sat heavy in my jaw. Grief pulled at the base of my throat. And love — love spread quietly like warmth through my hands.

Learning to Listen

Healing the past through the present begins with listening. Not analyzing or fixing, but simply noticing what the body has been trying to tell you all along.

Try this: Place a hand over your heart. Close your eyes. Breathe deeply three times — in through the nose, out through the mouth. Ask your body, *"What are you holding for me?"* Then wait. Maybe you'll feel a tingle, a weight, or nothing at all. Whatever arises, thank it. The body doesn't speak in words; it speaks in feeling. Gratitude is how it learns that it's finally safe to speak.

When you make a practice of listening, your body begins to trust you again. The tension slowly unwinds. The breath deepens. The heartbeat steadies. And without any dramatic moment, the past begins to loosen its grip.

A Moment of Release

I remember once sitting quietly after a long day — the kind of stillness that feels like surrender. Out of nowhere, tears began to fall. They weren't tied to a thought, only a deep, physical release. It was as if my body had been holding its breath for years and finally exhaled.

That moment didn't erase the past, but it transformed my relationship with it. It taught me that healing doesn't require understanding every detail — only being willing to feel what the body already knows.

Reflection — The Sacred Messenger

The body is not the enemy of the spirit; it is its messenger. Every ache, flutter, and tremor is an invitation to meet the past with tenderness. When we learn to feel without fear, the past stops haunting and starts harmonizing.

Affirmation

"My body is not my cage — it is my compass. Every sensation leads me closer to peace."

Journaling Prompts

1. When does your body feel most tense, and what might it be protecting you from?

2. Describe a time when you felt emotion physically (goosebumps, heaviness, warmth). What was your body telling you?

3. How can you show your body appreciation today for all it has carried?

Journaling

Journaling

Chapter 10 — Presence as Medicine

"The present moment is where time forgives itself."

The Gift of Now

When we talk about healing the past, we often imagine going back — revisiting old memories, tracing pain to its source. But what if healing doesn't require traveling backward at all? What if peace is found by standing *so fully* in the present that the past can finally rest?

For years, I believed I had to keep searching, keep digging into what happened, who said what, who hurt whom. But the more I tried to fix the past, the more I stayed bound by it. It was only when I began grounding myself in *this* moment — this breath, this light, this quiet heartbeat — that I realized: the present is the only place where change can actually occur.

Right now is where the body softens, the heart releases, and time folds back into harmony. The day I wrote these words, a message found me about time folding onto itself. It felt like confirmation — that healing in the present truly does ripple backward, touching what once seemed unreachable. Maybe synchronicity is simply the universe whispering, "See? You've already begun."

The Medicine of Ordinary Moments

Sometimes healing doesn't look like meditation or ritual. Sometimes it looks like folding laundry. Like stirring soup. Like sitting with a cup of tea while the sun shifts through the window. Each small act of awareness says, *"I'm here. I'm safe. Life can be simple again."*

I began to treat my daily tasks as medicine — little moments of presence that stitched calm back into the fabric of my life. When I sewed, I listened to the hum of the machine as though it were a prayer. When I scrapbooked, I watched the evolving pages as though it were the earth whispering back. And slowly, the past lost its power to define me.

Presence is not about escape; it's about returning to this breath, this heartbeat, this moment of being alive.

Anchoring Practice

Try this simple exercise whenever you feel pulled into old stories or future fears:

1. **Pause.** Notice where you are — the sounds, the air, the light.

2. **Breathe.** Inhale through the nose for a count of four, exhale through the mouth for six. Feel the exhale release not just air but tension.

3. **Name three things** around you that bring comfort or beauty: a candle flame, a favorite mug, the rhythm of your breath.

4. **Whisper:** *"This moment is enough."*

You may not feel instant serenity — but each time you return to now, you loosen another thread of the past's hold.

Time as a Circle

The more I practiced being present, the more I began to sense that time isn't a straight line but a circle — one that breathes with us. When I rest in the now, I feel my ancestors resting too. When I forgive, I feel old echoes softening. It's as if healing in the present sends ripples both forward and backward, smoothing the waters on which our lineage travels.

The mind can't explain it — but the heart feels it. And maybe that's all that's needed.

Reflection — The Quiet Cure

Peace doesn't come from solving the past; it comes from letting the present hold it. Each mindful moment is a balm that seeps through generations, teaching the soul that safety is possible.

Affirmation

"I am here, and that is enough. Each breath I take heals what time once held."

Journaling Prompts

1. What everyday moments bring you back into calm awareness?

2. When do you notice yourself drifting into the past — and how does returning to the present feel?

3. What does "being here now" mean for your healing journey today?

Journaling

Journaling

Chapter 11 — Rewriting the Story

"When we change the story, we change the spell."

The Power of the Words We Tell

Every family has its stories. Some are told with laughter, some whispered in warning, and others carried quietly — too heavy to name aloud. For years, I didn't realize how those stories were shaping me. I believed what I'd been told — that we were cursed, that misfortune ran in our blood, that happiness was something other families were born into.

But language is living energy. Every word spoken about who we are becomes a seed, and the stories we repeat are the gardens we grow. When we speak of pain as permanent, we give it roots. When we speak of healing as possible, we give it wings.

From Curse to Calling

There came a point when I couldn't bear to repeat the same lines anymore — the ones about struggle, loss, and never being enough. So, I began to rewrite them. Not on paper at first, but in the way I thought, the way I spoke, the way I responded to life.

I stopped calling it a curse and started calling it an invitation — a chance for the soul to evolve through experience. Once I saw it that way, the pattern changed. Instead of running from my family story, I began to understand that my task wasn't to escape it, but to *transform it.*

Healing the past through the present is not about erasing what was written — it's about becoming the author who adds the next chapter.

The Alchemy of Language

Words are frequency. When you tell your story with compassion instead of bitterness, the vibration shifts. When you choose "lesson" instead of "punishment," the entire body softens in recognition of truth.

Try saying aloud:

- "I was never cursed; I was chosen to bring awareness."

- "My ancestors weren't broken; they were learning to be whole."

- "Their pain was the soil where my peace would grow."

The words you choose reshape your timeline. They turn old energy into new life.

The Letter of Release

If you wish, take a blank page and write a letter to your ancestors, to your younger self, or even to the energy of the past itself. Begin with honesty. Say what hurt, what lingered, what never made sense. Then, as you continue, shift toward forgiveness and gratitude. End with a promise:

"I release you from my story, and I release myself from yours. We are free to love each other in peace."

You don't have to send it or read it aloud. The act of writing it is enough. Each word becomes an offering, a key turning in a lock that has waited generations to open.

Reflection — The Pen That Heals

Rewriting the story doesn't deny the pain; it redeems it. It turns the narrative of suffering into a map of strength, reminding us that even the most challenging journeys can lead home. When we tell the story differently, the ending changes — not only for us, but for all who came before.

Affirmation

"I am the author of my becoming. The story changes because I tell it with love."

Journaling Prompts

1. What story about your life or family do you find yourself repeating — and how could you tell it differently now?

2. If you were to write a new chapter for your lineage, what would its title be?

3. What does forgiveness sound like when you write it in your own words?

Journaling

Journaling

Chapter 12 — The Circle of Mothers

"Through every mother who came before me, I am born again in compassion."

The Lineage of Women

There's a thread that runs through every generation of women — invisible but strong, woven from love, endurance, and longing. Each mother passes down more than her eyes or voice; she passes her fears, her hopes, and her unfinished dreams. Some of those dreams take root. Others lie dormant, waiting for a daughter who will finally give them light.

I think often of my mother and the two women who followed her — the mothers I gained through love and marriage. Each arrived in a different season of my life, each carrying her own lessons, her own way of nurturing. Together they form a circle — one that taught me that "mother" is not a single role, but a presence that reappears whenever love is ready to grow.

My Mother's Hands

My mother's hands were always busy — cooking, cleaning, worrying. Even when they rested, they held tension, as if they feared what might happen if they ever let go. She lived her life in service to everyone else's needs, rarely her own. For a long time, I mistook that for weakness. Now I see it for what it was — devotion without guidance, love without self-permission.

She didn't know how to make life soft, but she gave me the desire to learn how. And that desire became the beginning of healing.

My First Mother-in-Law's Gift

When my mother passed, life fell into a stillness that frightened me. Then came my first mother-in-law — patient, warm, quietly wise. She never tried to replace what I'd lost; she simply stood beside it. With her I learned small acts of beauty: how to sew, how to turn scraps of fabric into something that could last. Looking back, I realize she was showing me the art of re-creation — how a woman can build love out of whatever remains.

Her hands taught what my mother's heart couldn't: that tenderness is also strength.

The Mother Who Came Later

Years later, after my life had turned new pages and love had found me again, another mother entered my story. By then, I was no longer a young woman searching for guidance, but one who had begun to understand her own path. My second mother-in-law met me where I was — wiser, softer, more whole. We shared friendship more than instruction, understanding more than obligation. Through her, I learned that the circle of mothers never truly ends; it simply widens, making room for every soul who loves with grace.

Her presence reminded me that life continues to offer nurturing, even when we think we've outgrown it.

What touched me most about her was her heart for harmony. With four sons, each so different, she often found herself standing in the quiet space between them — the steady center in a swirl of strong personalities. More than once, she told me how she prays that when she is gone, her boys will continue to love one another, to speak kindly, to stay connected. Her prayer isn't just for them; it's for all families who struggle to remain whole. She reminds me that peace within a family is not accidental — it's tended like a garden, watered with patience, and guarded by prayer.

Through her, I've come to see that keeping peace is also an act of courage. It is the sacred work of the heart.

The Ritual of Three Flames

To honor them — my mother, and the two mothers-by-marriage who followed — I light three candles. One for the pain that taught me. One for the love that remained. And one for the wisdom that arrived later, steady and calm. When the flames burn together, they lean toward one another as if in quiet conversation — a trinity of guidance whispering across time.

That, I think, is how healing works: we don't erase the sorrow; we let it sit beside the joy until both burn brighter.

The Circle Expands

Now, when I look at the women in my life — daughters, sisters, friends — I see that same lineage continuing, transformed. Where my mother felt trapped, I see choice. Where my first mother-in-law saw possibility, I see creation. Where my second mother-in-law offered calm, I see peace that stays. And I realize that the circle of mothers isn't limited by blood; it's made of every soul who teaches us how to love more gently.

To honor them is to live differently — to stop the inheritance of self-denial and begin the legacy of compassion.

Reflection — The Feminine Thread

The healing of the mother line is the healing of the world. Every time a woman forgives herself, speaks kindly to her reflection, or dares to rest, she rewrites history for all who came before her. We do not heal alone; we heal in a circle.

Affirmation

"Through the women who shaped me, I learned endurance. Through the woman I am becoming, I bring peace to them all."

Journaling Prompts

1. What lessons — spoken or unspoken — did you inherit from the women in your family?

2. How can you honor both the pain and the love that were passed down to you?

3. Who in your life today continues to embody the energy of "mother" for you, and how can you thank her?

Journaling

Journaling

Chapter 13 — The Fathers and the Forgiveness of Silence

"Even silence, when understood, becomes its own kind of love."

The Weight of Quiet Men

My father was a quiet man — not cold, just contained. He came from a world where feelings were folded neatly away, tucked behind work and duty. His hands spoke louder than his words ever did: the steady way he held a hammer, the long hours he gave to a job that asked more than it offered, the glass of highball that ended each day like a small, private ritual.

I used to think silence was indifference. Now I understand it was survival — the only language his generation of men was allowed to speak. They were taught that endurance was love, that providing was protection, and that needing comfort was weakness.

I sometimes wonder what my father would have been like if he had been born in gentler times — if he had been allowed to rest, to cry, to laugh without guilt. Maybe he would have known that silence can be lifted, not just carried.

Unspoken Love

He never said the words, *I'm proud of you,* but I remember how he'd fix what was broken without being asked. How he made sure the car had gas before we left. How he'd come home exhausted, yet still make sure we had what we needed.

In those small gestures, I've learned to recognize what he couldn't say aloud. Love wears many shapes. Some are loud and lyrical. Others are quiet as a man sitting in his chair after a long day, exhaling the only peace he knows.

The Fathers Before Him

My father's story wasn't his alone. He came from men who had known hard work and more challenging times — men who crossed oceans, who shoveled coal to stay warm, who enlisted before they were old enough to shave. They, too, were shaped by duty, not tenderness. And maybe that's why their love became so practical — a roof, a meal, a job done well — even when their hearts longed to say more.

To understand my father, I had to see them too: a long line of men doing their best with the tools they were given. It wasn't lack of love that silenced them; it was the weight of expectation.

Healing the Masculine Line

There comes a moment in healing when we must forgive not just others, but the collective silence itself — the generations of fathers who never learned the language of softness. Forgiveness doesn't mean excusing harm; it means releasing ourselves from the hardness that silence creates.

When I think of my father now, I don't see the man who couldn't express his feelings. I see the boy who was put in an orphanage, who shoveled coal until his hands blistered, who enlisted at sixteen, and who carried that toughness like armor his entire life. He did what he knew. And somehow, that's enough.

The more I heal, the more I sense him resting — not gone, just quieter still, as though relieved that I can finally hear what he never could say.

Reflection — Love Beneath the Quiet

The men before us were taught to love in silence, to give through doing, and to hold emotion until it burned away. When we listen closely, their silence becomes something else — not absence, but an offering. They endured so we could become the ones who speak, soften, and stay.

Affirmation

"I honor the men who came before me. Their silence shaped me, but it does not define me. I forgive the quiet and hear the love within it."

Journaling Prompts

1. What lessons did the men in your family teach you — through both words and silence?

2. When have you mistaken someone's quietness for indifference? What might have been underneath it?

3. How can you bring gentleness to the masculine energy within yourself — the part that protects, provides, and endures?

Journaling

Journaling

Chapter 14 — The Language of Energy

"Everything we are is vibration waiting to be remembered."

The Invisible Thread

There's a current that runs through everything — through thought, emotion, memory, and time itself. We can't see it, but we feel it in the spaces between words, in the shiver that rises during truth, in the quiet hum of a room where love once lived. Energy is the soul's handwriting — invisible ink that reveals itself only to those who learn to see softly.

Long before I understood what "energy" meant, I felt it. When someone walked into a room, I could sense their mood before they spoke. When my mother was upset, the air itself seemed to tighten. And when I began to heal, the world started to feel lighter — as though the unseen had been waiting for me to notice that it was part of me, not separate.

The Frequency of Emotion

Each emotion carries a vibration. Fear trembles fast and high, anxiety buzzing like static. Grief moves slowly, heavy, like thunder rolling across water. Peace hums low and steady — the sound of breath, the rhythm of ocean waves. Love, though — love has no single tone. It is the harmony that makes all others meaningful.

When we hold pain too long, it stagnates — becoming dense energy in the body. But when we allow it to move — through tears, breath, or creation — it transforms. That is the alchemy of feeling: energy becoming light again.

Healing Through Resonance

When you begin to live in awareness of energy, you learn that what you give your attention to grows stronger. A thought, repeated often enough, becomes a vibration. A vibration, felt long enough, becomes a reality.

Healing the past through the present means choosing which frequencies to amplify — compassion over resentment, gratitude over regret, faith over fear. It's not denial; it's direction. You turn your dial toward light until the static fades.

One of the simplest ways to shift energy is through breath. Breathe in peace. Breathe out release. Breathe until the rhythm in your chest matches the rhythm of the earth beneath your feet.

You don't have to "try" to heal; the body and soul know how to realign once the noise quiets.

Time, Folded by Frequency

The more I attuned to the subtle, the more I understood that time isn't fixed — it's fluid, responding to vibration. When I release anger today, I feel generations behind me sigh in relief. When I choose love instead of fear, the future softens in response. Healing, then, is not linear — it's resonant. Each act of presence sends ripples through the spiral of time, harmonizing what was once dissonant.

That is the secret language of energy: it doesn't speak in words, but in echoes. And every echo knows how to find its way home.

A Simple Realignment Practice

Find a quiet moment. Place one hand over your heart, the other over your solar plexus. Close your eyes. Take three slow breaths.

Now, silently repeat: "I am light remembering itself." Notice any sensations — warmth, tingling, calm, or even tears. Don't judge them; they're just the body's way of translating energy into feeling. Stay for a moment, letting breath and awareness weave into one gentle rhythm.

When you open your eyes, take note of how colors seem clearer, sounds softer, and time slower. That's alignment — not an escape from reality, but an entry into its truest form.

Reflection — The Music Beneath the Noise

We are all instruments in the same great symphony. When we tune ourselves to peace, we help the whole world find harmony. The work of energy healing is to remember that every vibration — even pain — is seeking to return to love.

Affirmation

"I am a vessel of living energy. Each breath restores balance to my past, peace to my present, and light to my future."

Journaling Prompts

1. When do you most notice the energy around or within you shifting — for better or worse?

2. What helps you return to peace when you feel surrounded by tension or heaviness?

3. How does it feel to imagine your healing sending ripples backward and forward through time?

Journaling

Journaling

Chapter 15 — Creating Through Healing

"What heals you will eventually ask to be shared."

The Return of Creation

Healing does not end with stillness; it moves again — this time through the hands, the voice, the imagination. There comes a point when peace inside the heart begins to overflow, and creation becomes its natural language. That is how the soul celebrates recovery: not by forgetting what hurt it, but by transforming it into beauty.

When I first began writing and creating again, I didn't realize that I was documenting my own rebirth. Each word, each line I painted, each scrapbook I created carried the quiet message: *I am still here, and I am whole.* The work itself became prayer — proof that love can build something new out of what was once broken.

The Art of Transformation

For me, creativity didn't arrive in a single burst; it returned softly, the way sunlight creeps across a room. It began with small things — sewing fabric into gifts, making soaps for others, writing reflections that I wasn't sure anyone would read. Those humble acts became altars of intention.

Each creation carried vibration — the energy of joy, of care, of quiet devotion. It didn't matter whether it was a book, a journal, or a simple label design; what mattered was that each thing I made carried a frequency of love. And love, as I'd learned, heals everything it touches.

That's when I realized creativity is not just expression; it's medicine.

Rooted Hound as Renewal

When Rooted Hound Press was born, it wasn't only a business — it was a declaration of wholeness. It said, *My roots are deep. My spirit is awake. My voice has value.* Every project, every poem, every page was another step in turning pain into purpose.

What had once felt like the "curse" of struggle became the catalyst for building something sacred — a place where stories, wisdom, and beauty could live together. Through creation, I wasn't just healing myself; I was extending healing to others. Each book became a mirror for someone else's remembering.

In that way, creation is a form of generosity — a way of saying, *I've walked this path. Let me light it for you, too.*

The Creative Frequency

Creation holds vibration. When we make something with intention — even the smallest act — we send out a signal that shifts the energy around us. Cooking a meal with gratitude, writing a letter with love, planting a flower in honor of an ancestor — all of it becomes prayer in motion.

To create through healing means to stay connected to the present moment while allowing the soul's memory to flow through the hands. That is the true alchemy — spirit made tangible.

A Simple Practice: Creating with Intention

The next time you create — anything at all — pause before you begin. Close your eyes. Take one slow breath. Whisper:

"May this carry light." Then begin. Let the action itself be meditation. Notice the textures, the colors, the sounds. Feel your breath guiding the rhythm. When you finish, hold your creation for a moment and offer it a silent thank-you — for what it gave to you as you made it.

That's how energy completes its circle: what heals you becomes healing for others.

Reflection — The Art of Becoming

Creation is how the soul remembers it is limitless. It's how grief turns into beauty, and beauty turns into belonging. When we make something with love, we're not just shaping matter; we're shaping meaning. And meaning is what keeps the light alive long after we're gone.

Affirmation

"I create with love and purpose. My art, my words, my life — all are vessels of healing."

Journaling Prompts

1. What forms of creativity bring you peace or joy?

2. How has your own healing inspired you to make or share something new?

3. What message would you want your creations to whisper to others long after you're gone?

Journaling

Journaling

Chapter 16 — Living the Blessing Forward

"Healing becomes complete when it turns into generosity."

Becoming the Blessing

There comes a moment in every healing journey when we realize we're no longer walking to escape pain — we're walking to carry light.

The past no longer pulls from behind; it pushes gently from beneath, like earth supporting every step. That's when healing becomes something larger than ourselves — not a destination, but a living blessing.

I used to wonder what "purpose" meant. Was it a career, a calling, some divine mission written in the stars? Now I understand that purpose isn't always grand; sometimes it's quiet. It's the way we speak softly when others shout. It's choosing patience where anger once lived. It's continuing to love in a world that often forgets how.

Living the blessing forward means letting your wholeness become someone else's hope.

The Ripples of Light

Every time we heal a pattern within ourselves — every time we respond with understanding instead of judgment, or compassion instead of defense — we send a ripple backward through our ancestry and forward through the generations yet to come. Healing multiplies. Love compounds. Peace travels farther than we'll ever see.

I like to imagine those ripples moving through time like light refracting in water — touching every soul connected to ours. Perhaps that's how the universe mends itself: one peaceful heart at a time.

So I live my life as prayer in motion — not perfect, not constant, but sincere. Every candle I pour, every book I write, every word of encouragement I speak is a ripple of remembrance: *We are not broken. We are becoming.*

The Sacred Exchange

True healing doesn't hoard what it learns; it gives it away. When we offer our experience to others — not as advice, but as presence — we become part of the great exchange of grace. It's not about teaching people how to heal; it's about showing them what healed energy feels like.

A healed person brings calm into chaos. A healed voice speaks truth without harm. A healed heart doesn't need to prove its worth — it radiates it. That is living the blessing: to walk as evidence that peace is possible.

The Legacy of Love

One day, long after we're gone, our children or their children will feel something they can't quite name — a quiet strength in their bones, a calm they didn't earn, a hope that seems to appear from nowhere.

That will be us — the echo of our healing carried forward.

Our ancestors left us the work of survival. We leave our descendants the gift of peace. That is legacy.

To live whole is to plant seeds we may never see bloom — trusting that love will find its way through the soil of time.

Reflection — The Continuation of Light

Healing is not the end of the story; it is the beginning of the blessing. When we live from peace, every ordinary moment becomes holy. Each kindness, each creation, each prayer is an offering that sustains the world a little longer. The light we carry was never meant to be kept — it was meant to be passed on.

Affirmation

"I am the living proof of my lineage's healing. The peace I embody becomes their peace too. I live my blessing forward, with gratitude and grace."

Journaling Prompts

1. In what ways has your healing already touched others — even quietly or unexpectedly?

2. What does "living your blessing forward" look like in daily life for you?

3. If future generations could receive one message from your life, what would it be?

Epilogue — The Bridge of Light

"The past no longer haunts me; it walks beside me — healed, remembered, and free."

A Letter Across Time

If I could send a letter through the folds of time, I would send it to all of you — to the mother who prayed through her tears, to the father who carried his love in silence, to the ancestors who wandered foreign soil believing they'd lost everything, and to the girl I once was, sitting in the shadow of their stories, wondering if life could ever feel safe.

I would tell you that it all mattered. Every ache, every loss, every attempt to love in the only way you knew how — none of it was wasted. It all became the soil from which peace would one day bloom.

I used to think healing meant undoing what came before. Now I know it means *embracing it until it no longer hurts.*

The River Between Worlds

There are days I still feel you near — in a song that drifts through the air, in the flicker of candlelight, in the warmth that rises unbidden when I speak your names.

You are not gone. You have crossed the river of time, and I have built a bridge of light to meet you there. Each act of forgiveness became a plank. Each prayer was a beam. Each moment of love is the glow that keeps it visible through the fog.

We meet there now — not in pain, but in peace. And together we watch the ripples of healing stretch outward, touching everyone who will ever come from our line.

And sometimes I think of that Princess — the one whose pride cast a shadow through generations. I no longer see her as a villain, but as a wounded girl whose heart broke in silence. Perhaps all this time she, too, has been waiting to be forgiven. Maybe that forgiveness, offered through love and understanding, was what finally broke the curse — not for her, not for me, but for us both.

To My Mother

You taught me what it means to endure, and through you, I learned that strength without softness is only half the story. I wish I could have shown you what I know now — that life was always waiting to be beautiful for you, that peace was never as far away as it felt. But I believe that you know now. And when I feel you near — in the hum of dragonfly wings or the soft glow of morning light — I sense your joy, at last unburdened.

You are free. And so am I.

To My Father

Your silence used to ache like absence, but I understand it now — it was your armor, your way of loving through endurance. The world taught you to hold your pain behind steady hands, but you gave me the tools to build something more substantial: compassion, faith, and the courage to stay.

If you can hear me, know this — your story ended in peace, not regret. I've made sure of it.

To the Girl I Once Was

You did it. You turned every fear into faith. You learned to trust your own heart. You found love again — in people, in life, in yourself. And one day, you sat down to write it all, not to prove anything, but to remember.

I know now that every moment you thought was breaking, you were really shaping yourself into someone strong enough to hold the light. Thank you for never giving up.

To the Reader

You are part of this story now. By holding these words, you've stepped onto the bridge of light with me. Whatever you carry from your own past — the sorrow, the silence, the weight of things unhealed — know this: you have the power to rewrite it, to bless it, to set it free.

When you live your peace, you send ripples through time itself. And perhaps, someday, someone in your family line will pause, breathe, and feel a sudden calm — and that calm will be *you,* whispering through the folds of time: "It's all right now. We made it home."

And the bridge of light remains — not behind us, but within us.